Contents

Chapter

1	**Introduction**
2	**Step 1**
3	**Step 2**
4	**Step 3**
5	**Resources**

Risk Disclaimer

I have taken the utmost care in my research with regards to this eBook and as always with any financial investment or speculation your capital is at risk of loss and when trading you may lose more than your initial investment. The best advice I can give you is do not risk more than you are prepared to lose.

Regards
Paul Stanley

Introduction

I have written this book to increase the possibility of helping you escape the rat race, of 9 to 5 unfulfilling jobs and allowing you to be able to spend more time watching your family grow up and living in a financially comfortable and secure situation, spending your time enjoying life and having the money to lead a fulfilling semi retired existence; playing golf, reading, driving your convertible, going on fantastic foreign holidays, it's up to you!

Sounds like a dream, right?

Well I think you will be very interested in what I have to tell you in this book and I hope you will use it to help shape you and your family and friends futures.

This book is aimed at the unemployed, low income workers, full and part time employees, the self employed and people who are retired and need extra income.

In this book, I will give you an insight into how you can start to accumulate wealth and earn a steady income, without having to start out with a lot of money, to invest.

In fact I advise you to start off small and invest only £100 to get going.

Sounds too good to be true, right?

Well no, it isn't too good to be true or a false financial hope.

After many years of countless hours, trawling through the internet, I have discovered 2 great ways of earning a comfortable living, which requires an initial investment of only £100 and takes only 30 minutes to 2 hours a day of work, if you can call it work.

About Me

I have previously worked as a financial adviser, I have studied Business Management at the Open University and gained qualifications, and I truly believe that this book will set you on the path to financial freedom.

What this book will show you, with its 3 steps herein, is that you will never have to work again in your life or at least, you will see that it is possible to earn money with minimal investment outlay and minimal time from just 30 minutes a day.

So if you are interested in finding out about how to be free again, like when you were young, keep reading.

Step 1

Matched Betting, not Gambling!

What is matched betting?

Matched betting is a technique used by punters and bookmakers, to bet on an outcome of a sports event without risk.

Essentially there is no risk with matched betting as all possible outcomes are bet on.

Firstly, you have to make a back bet with online bookmakers:

E.g. Football fixture:

Manchester United v Chelsea

Back bet: Man United to win

Then you need to place another bet, known as a Lay bet on the only remaining possible outcomes left, so your lay bet would be:

Manchester United to lose or draw

i.e. you select Lay all against Man United in the exchange section of the Betfair.com website which is highlighted in Red.

Because football only has 3 possible outcomes i.e. win, lose or draw it is an ideal sport to bet on. So...

Back Bet

Man United to win against Chelsea (with bookmakers online)

Lay bet

Man United to lose or draw against Chelsea (with betfair or other betting exchange)

As you can see, the lay bet covers 2 possible outcomes and the back bet covers the other one.

The back bet can be made with any online bookmakers and the lay bet can be made on any betting exchange like betfair in the exchange section of the websites. Betting exchanges make it possible to cover 2 possible outcomes, lose or draw by selecting lay all (in this case against man united) in the right hand red column.

Because you have covered all possible outcomes of the football match, you are 99% likely to win because all angles are covered. I say 99% likely, because there is a chance you could lose, if you put the wrong figures or odds into the matched betting calculator.

A matched betting calculator should always be used, so that you can see the potential win or loss for both parts of the bet. i.e. the Back bet and Lay bet.

When using the matched betting calculator, you need to enter the detaisl of the back bet. i.e.

(Man United to Win)
Stake: £10   Odds (in decimal) 6

Then you need to enter the lay bet odds in decimal which you can find on betfair or other betting exchange, for the fixture. i.e.

Man United
Lay All Odds (in decimal) 1.46

Once entered in the calculator, it will tell you the amount of money you need to fund the lay bet which is the Liability Amount (this is how much you are risking in the lay bet.)

To get the correct figures in the Lay bet you must enter the Lay amount as told by the matched betting calculator and your liability should then match on the calculator and on the betting exchange. If it doesn't, check over your figures again.

The calculator will then show you, how much of a profit or loss will occur for all outcomes of which your two bets cover. The back bet and lay bets win, lose with either one, should balance.

The calculator program is written based on a mathematical equation, that calculates how much the lay bet should be given the stake amount and taking into account, the odds for both sides of the bet, i.e. the back bet and lay bet.

Matched betting is possible because of the math's and probability coverage of the outcomes which are covered 100%, also by using free bet offers from Online UK bookmakers, it is easy to make a profit.

There is a free matched betting calculator on www.profitaccumulator.co.uk and www.oddsmonkey.co.uk.

The profit potential of matched betting can be enough to be a sole source of income.

When taking advantage of free bet offers, you first usually, need to make a qualifying bet.

E.g.

>£5 bet on Coral
>GIVES YOU
>4 X Free £5 bets

So you can then make 4 profitable bets free because of the coral offer and you can cover each these bets with a lay bet on betfair or another betting exchange.

Sign Up offers with Bookmakers

Many online UK bookmakers offer free bets to encourage more people to bet and use their services. Currently there are over 100 offers available from UK bookmakers online. So take advantage of these free bets and offers to guarantee a profit.

Remember: Always use a Matched Betting Calculator!

The matched betting calculator has two other features besides its main job, these are:

A bet profitability score in % which is good for comparing bet to bet.

Also you can specify if the matched bet is a standard bet, a free bet (stake not returned) or a free bet (stake returned.) Usually the free bet will be of the stake not returned type.

The results from these calculators are very accurate as you can enter any back or lay bet commission that you're charge by the bookmaker or betting exchange.

Summary

Pros:

100% Success probability

£100 only to start

Able to reinvest profits for future greater profits

Only 30 minutes to 2 hours a day needed.

Cons:

Error whilst input the odds, into the matched betting calculator, could create inaccurate results and financial loss.

Always remember to enter the odds into the calculator in decimal form!

Step 2

Investment

In order to progress onto the third and final stage, using the matched betting techniques from step 1 to develop income, it is necessary to accumulate £10 to 15K in your bank account.

There are several ways that this sum can be achieved, though it will take up to 2 years of investing.

For example; If you invested £300 a month and earned 10 % interest per year, it would take just under 3 years to raise £10K.

In the United Kingdom, the most tax efficient way to invest is via a stocks and shares ISA (Individual Savings Account.)

An ISA is an investment wrapper that allows your funds to be free from Capital Gains Tax and Income Tax, though you will have to pay stamp duty on your investments that are in the ISA.

The current annual limit to the amount you can invest is £20K per year in 2021/22.

If you do not live in the UK, you can invest in Unit trusts which are a similar investment, but you will have to abide by your own countries tax rules.

The best way to achieve a decent return on your investment is to invest in either a actively managed fund, or an index tracker fund.

An actively managed fund is run by investment bankers with the main aim of beating the returns of the general stock market or fund sector by actively buying and selling shares (stocks) instead of just holding on to the shares and increasing the amount.

An Index Tracker fund, aims to mirror the stock market E.G. FTSE100 or All share index by investing in the full range of shares (stocks) in proportions that make up the FTSE All Share index or FTSE100. These shares are not actively managed.

There are pros and cons which can dictate which type of fund will suit your circumstances but that is better covered by other books as I do not wish to give specific investment advice.

Step 2 is mainly written, to get you thinking about the future and investments in general.

Actively managed or Index Tracker funds will usually be based on funds by geographical location, sector type or a specific stock market index.

E.g. North American Fund (Geographical)
Tech Fund (Sector type)
FTSE All Share Tracker (stock market index.)

The main reason that I am suggesting that you invest or consider investing in a stock and shares ISA or a Unit trust is because historically, stock market investment usually out perform all other investments except maybe property, over the medium to long term i.e. 5 years plus.

Returns averaging 10% a year are achievable over 5 years.

The important thing to remember when investing in Unit Trusts and ISA's is that past performance is no guarantee of future performance and that your investment value will fluctuate.

When investing for the medium term, i.e. 5 years, it is important to realize that the money invested is of a low liquidity, compared to cash which is of high liquidity.

It is important when investing to make regular deposits on a monthly basis and only liquidate your investment when you have £10 to £15K in your fund.

Don't sell when your unit values or shares are low, use the fluctuation as an opportunity to buy more units or shares when the price is low.

The main thing is not to panic or succumb to your emotions.

I strongly advise that you consult an Independent Financial Consultant (IFA) when considering any investment.

You could alternatively, consult a tied financial adviser, but they will only be able to recommend financial funds or products that are available from their company, where as an Independent Financial Adviser can advise you on a wider range of products and give you unbiased advice. They will however, charge you a fee for their advise, which is how they make their money.

A tied adviser will usually be paid by commission on the sales of their companies products and maybe more likely to sell you products that they earn themselves greater commission on.

Summary

This chapter should always be used as a foundation or basis for good financial management, by investing for the future and it will always be relevant to your future prosperity whether you are on step 1 or 3 of this book.

Please bear in mind that investing an amount on a monthly basis will benefit your investments more by compounding the interest and additionally you will also benefit from pound cost averaging, which is when you purchase units at a lower average when compared to a yearly on off investment deposit.

STEP 3

Hedge Fund Trading Style

Once you've accumulated £10k to £15K in your bank account you will then have the opportunity to generate a very good income, using a method that Hedge Fund managers use to make income in any market conditions, be it up, down or sideways (static) in trend.

This technique put simply, if you forgive the pun, is Put writing.

So what is a Put and how do you write one?

A Put is a type of options contract that enables the buyer of an asset (which could be a commodity or stocks and shares) to sell a set number of the asset at a specific price which is known as the strike price, at a pre determined, later date. The trader isn't obligated exercise the option.

Usually someone would buy a Put option contract because they expect the assets price to decrease during the time that the option is valid for. They purchase the Put option for a fee, known as the Premium.

If the stock goes up in value when compared to the option strike price, the trader will not exercise the option and their only loss is the premium they paid for the contract.

If however, trader that has bought the Put option is correct and the stock goes down, the trader will make a profit, provided that the strike price+premium is more than the spot price, i.e. the current market price.

So what is put writing then?

Put writing is when you write or sell a put contract to a trader for which you will immediately receive the Premium within minutes in to your trading account. This can then be withdrawn to your bank account.

When you write a Put option contract you do so with the expectation of the value of the underlying asset, share or stock going up.

In such a situation, the buyer of your contract will forfeit the premium they paid you for the contract as they would not exercise it.

The main reason that this is a good way to generate income is that if done correctly, Put writing gives you the premium to keep 85% of the time because usually the contracts aren't exercised by the trader that has bought it from you.

The main thing to understand is that you need £10k to £15k in your account so that you are allowed to write the Put and cover it with your funds.

If the trader that buys the Put contract from you exercises the Put then you are under the obligation to buy the shares or stock from the trader at the strike price.

The second thing to remember is to only write Put contracts on share or stocks that you would like to own, just in case you need to honor the contract.

Using this method of Writing Puts with £10k to £15k to cover them, it is easily possible to generate an income of £3000 a month, with a minimal time outlay of 5 to 10 minutes per week.

Finally, this method of income generation can be done anywhere in the world with an internet connection.

Resources

Matched Betting

www.profitaccumulator.co.uk

www.oddsmonkey.com

Betting Exchanges

www.betfair.com

www.smarkets.com

www.betdaq.com

www.sports.ladbrokes.com

Options Brokers

www.home.saxo

www.ig.com

Fin

www.ingramcontent.com/pod-product-compliance
Lightning Source LLC
Chambersburg PA
CBHW070915220526
45466CB00005B/2223